FABULOUS ANIMALS

The Story of the Platypus

Anita Ganeri

raintree

a Capstone company — publishers for children

Raintree is an imprint of Capstone Global Library Limited, a company incorporated in England and Wales having its registered office at 264 Banbury Road, Oxford OX2 7DY – Registered company number: 6695582

www.raintree.co.uk
myorders@raintree.co.uk

Edited by Linda Staniford
Designed by Philippa Jenkins
Original illustrations © Capstone Global Library Limited 2016
Picture research by Morgan Walters
Production by Victoria Fitzgerald
Originated by Capstone Global Library Ltd
Printed and bound in China

ISBN 978 1 474 71452 5
19 18 17 16 15
10 9 8 7 6 5 4 3 2 1

British Library Cataloguing in Publication Data
A full catalogue record for this book is available from the British Library.

Acknowledgements
We would like to thank the following for permission to reproduce photographs: Alamy: INTERFOTO, 20, jackie ellis, 26, Kevin Wells, 12; Bridgeman Images: Nockels, David (20th century)/Private Collection /Look and Learn, 18; Getty Images: De Agostini Picture Library, 8; National Geographic Creative: JASON EDWARDS, 23; Newscom: D. Parer & E. Parer-Cook, 17, MICK TSIKAS/REUTERS, 15, Roland Seitre/Minden Pictures, 6, Roland Seitre/D. Parer & E. Parer-Cook/Minden Pictures, 16; Rebecca Pian, 27; Science Source: Jean-Philippe Varin, 19; Shutterstock: Aksenova Natalya, (duck head) 5, Curioso, (otter body) 5, Eric Isselee, (snake) bottom 7, Jagodka, (ferret) top 7, John Carnemolla, 9, Kletr, 25, kwest, 24, panbazil, (duck) middle 7; SuperStock: Minden Pictures, 13, NHPA, Cover, 10, 14, Universal Images Group, 11; Wikimedia: Freeman.pdf, 21, Wellcome Images, 4.

We would like to thank Michael Bright for his invaluable help in the preparation of this book.

Every effort has been made to contact copyright holders of material reproduced in this book. Any omissions will be rectified in subsequent printings if notice is given to the publisher.

All the internet addresses (URLs) given in this book were valid at the time of going to press. However, due to the dynamic nature of the internet, some addresses may have changed, or sites may have changed or ceased to exist since publication. While the author and publisher regret any inconvenience this may cause readers, no responsibility for any such changes can be accepted by either the author or the publisher.

Contents

Some words are shown in bold, like this.
You can find out what they mean by
looking in the glossary.

Mystery animal

In the 1700s, people from Britain began to settle in Australia. They saw many strange animals. Captain John Hunter was **Governor** of New South Wales. In 1798, he sent the skin of an extraordinary animal back to England.

Publ. by FP Nodder June 1799.

This is an early drawing of a platypus.

What sort of animal was this?

Scientists were puzzled. They thought that the animal must be a fake. It looked as if someone had sewn a duck's bill on to a **miniature** otter's body, with fur from a beaver.

More skins and skulls arrived from Australia. Scientists studied them carefully. They soon saw that this was a real animal after all. They called it the "platypus" which means "flat-footed", after its webbed feet.

A platypus has webbed feet for swimming.

For years, scientists tried to work out
what kind of animal it was.
It had fur like a **mammal**.

It had a bill like a bird.

It laid eggs like a bird or a **reptile**.

The scientists could not agree which group it
fitted into.

A new animal?

In 1883, a Scottish scientist, William Caldwell, arrived in Australia. He searched for platypus eggs and nests. He also caught a female that made milk for her babies. This proved that the platypus was a **monotreme** – a **mammal** that laid eggs.

This female platypus is in her nest with her eggs.

Like platypuses, echidnas are mammals that lay eggs.

Mammals are animals with fur or hair. They feed their babies on milk. Most mammals give birth to live babies but platypus babies hatch from eggs. The only other kind of monotremes are echidnas (spiny anteaters).

Local knowledge

Long before the Europeans came, the **indigenous** Australians hunted platypuses for their meat. They caught them in the water, using spears. Later, they helped scientists to look for platypuses.

A platypus comes out of its burrow.

The indigenous Australians also told stories about the platypus. One story tells how the mother of the first platypus was a duck. Its father was a water-rat. So, the platypus got its mother's bill and webbed feet, and its father's soft brown fur.

Meet the platypus

The platypus lives in rivers and streams in eastern Australia. It spends a lot of time in the water, looking for food. It digs burrows in the riverbank where it rests and makes its nest.

A platypus looks for food in the river.

Male platypuses have spurs on their back legs.

A platypus is about the size of a cat. Males are bigger than females. Males have little pointed **spurs** on their back legs. They use these to jab **venom** into **predators**, such as snakes, rats and **goannas**.

Platypus lifestyle

Platypuses are excellent swimmers. They use their webbed feet like paddles. They use their flat tails for steering. They close their eyes and ears underwater. But they have to come to the surface to breathe.

A platypus paddles with its webbed feet.

A platypus's special fur keeps it dry in the water.

A platypus has thick, brown fur on its body. The fur traps air next to its skin. This helps to keep the platypus warm in the water. Its fur is also waterproof.

A platypus eats worms, shrimps and insect grubs. It uses its bill to dig them up from the muddy riverbed. The platypus stores the food in pouches in its cheeks until it reaches the surface.

A platypus hunts for food on the riverbed.

The platypus's bill
is flat and smooth.

The platypus has special **sensors** in its
bill. It uses the sensors to find its food. Its
prey gives out tiny electrical signals. The
platypus's bill picks these signals up.

In October, the female platypus digs a special burrow in the riverbank. Inside, she builds a nest from grass and leaves. She lays two to three small, soft eggs in the nest. Then she curls around them to keep them warm.

A female platypus lays her eggs in her nest.

The babies hatch about 10 days later.
They have no hair and cannot see.
Their mother feeds them on milk. The
babies stay in the burrow until they
are about four months old.

In captivity

Scientists caught thousands of platypuses. But it was difficult to keep them alive for long. Then an Australian scientist, Henry Burrell, had a brilliant idea.

Scientists explored Australia in the 19th century.

Burrell called
his tank a
"platypusary".

In 1910, Burrell invented a special tank
for keeping platypuses. It had water and a
burrow inside to make the platypuses feel at
home. For the first time, Burrell caught some
platypuses and managed to keep them alive.

Some of the platypuses Henry Burrell caught were put on show at a zoo in Sydney. Then, in 1922, he helped to send a platypus to the Bronx Zoo in New York, USA. It was the first time a live platypus had been seen outside Australia.

Tickets like this were issued to see the platypuses in New York.

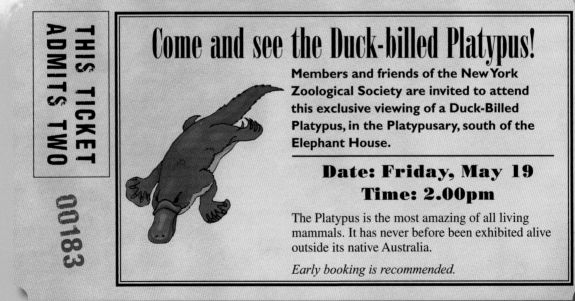

THIS TICKET
ADMITS TWO

00183

Come and see the Duck-billed Platypus!

Members and friends of the New York Zoological Society are invited to attend this exclusive viewing of a Duck-Billed Platypus, in the Platypusary, south of the Elephant House.

Date: Friday, May 19
Time: 2.00pm

The Platypus is the most amazing of all living mammals. It has never before been exhibited alive outside its native Australia.

Early booking is recommended.

These platypus twins were born in captivity.

Today, the only **captive** platypuses live in zoos in Australia. In 1998, a platypus at Healesville Sanctuary in Victoria gave birth to twins. They were named Barak and Yarra. These were the first platypus twins to be born in captivity.

Platypuses today

Today, platypuses still live in eastern Australia. A small group of platypuses also live on Kangaroo Island in South Australia. It is against the law to catch or trap a platypus.

Platypuses live on Kangaroo Island in Australia.

Groups, such as the Australian Platypus Conservancy, work hard to look after these amazing animals. One of their projects is to stop so many platypuses being accidentally caught and killed in **yabby** traps.

Scientists are still learning more about the platypus. In the 1980s and 1990s, scientists in Australia worked out how platypuses use the electrical **sensors** in their bills to search for food.

This scientist is on the look-out for platypuses.

Area for
Platypus viewing
& fishing

5 mm

This fossil tooth may come from the **ancestor** of the modern platypus.

In 2012, scientists in Australia found a fossil of a huge platypus tooth. They think that it comes from a giant platypus that lived around 5-15 million years ago. It looked similar to a modern platypus but was at least twice as big.

Platypus timeline

1798
John Hunter sends the first platypus skin to England.

1799
George Shaw writes the first scientific description of the platypus.

1803
Étienne Geoffroy St-Hilaire puts the platypus and echidna into the new animal group of monotremes.

1883/4
William Caldwell finds some platypus eggs, proving that this is an egg-laying mammal.

1910
Henry Burrell invents and builds his "platypusary".

1922

The first platypus outside Australia arrives at the Bronx Zoo, New York.

1943

David Fleay breeds "Corrie", the first platypus born in captivity at Healesville Sanctuary, Victoria, Australia.

1986

Scientists discover how the platypus uses its "electrical sense".

1998

The first platypus twins in captivity are born at Healesville Sanctuary.

2012

Scientists find a fossil of a tooth that belonged to a giant ancient platypus.

Glossary

ancestor family member who lived a very long time ago

captive animal that lives in a zoo or wildlife park

goanna type of lizard that lives in Australia

Governor official who ran parts of Australia on behalf of the British

indigenous native to a place

mammal warm-blooded animal that breathes air; mammals have hair or fur; female mammals feed milk to their young

miniature much smaller than usual size

monotreme mammal that lays eggs

platypusary special tank for keeping platypuses

predator animal that hunts other animals for food

prey animal that is hunted by another animal for food

reptile cold-blooded animal that breathes air and has a backbone; most reptiles lay eggs and have scaly skin

sensor part of an animal's body that detects changes in the world around it

spur spine-like bump on a platypus's leg

venom poison injected through an animal's bite or sting

yabby animal like a crayfish that lives in rivers and streams in Australia

Find out more

Books
Animals in Danger in Australia, Richard and Louise Spilsbury (Raintree, 2013)

Platypus, Sara Antill (Unusual Animals) (Windmill Books, 2010)

Super Natural Animals, Leon Gray (Wayland, 2014)

Websites
animals.nationalgeographic.com/animals/mammals/platypus
Find out more about the platypus on this site.

www.bbc.co.uk/nature/life/Platypus
This site gives information, photos and videos about the life and behaviour of the platypus.

www.zoo.org.au/healesville/animals/platypus
Meet the platypuses of Healesville Sanctuary in Australia and learn about platypus care.

Index